GLOBAL CITIZENSHIP

Improving the Quality of Life

A⁺

SUSAN WATSON

Smart Apple Media
1980 Lookout Drive
North Mankato
Minnesota 56003

Library of Congress Cataloging-in-Publication Data

Watson, Susan, 1949–
    Improving the quality of life / by Susan Watson.
    p. cm. — (Global citizenship)

    Includes index.
    Summary: Explores how the quality of life varies in different parts of the world and what can be done to help meet people's basic needs, both through government action and the efforts of individual citizens.

    ISBN 1-58340-403-1
    1. Quality of life—Juvenile literature. 2. Basic needs—Juvenile literature. 3. World citizenship—Juvenile literature.
    4. Globalization—Juvenile literature. [1. Quality of life. 2. Basic needs. 3. World citizenship. 4. Globalization.] I. Title.
    HN25. W38 2003
    306—dc21

                                                                                                    2002044627

First Edition
9 8 7 6 5 4 3 2 1

First published in 2003 by
MACMILLAN EDUCATION AUSTRALIA PTY LTD
627 Chapel Street, South Yarra, Australia 3141

Associated companies and representatives throughout the world.

Copyright © Susan Watson 2003

Packaged for Macmillan Education Australia by Publishing Options Pty Ltd
Text design by Gail McManus Graphics
Cover design by Dimitrios Frangoulis
Illustrations by Infographics Pty Ltd
Page make-up by Crackerjack Desktop Services

Printed in Thailand

Acknowledgements
The author is especially grateful to Matthew, Kyja, CJ, and Samantha for being the model global citizens of this series. The author and the publisher are grateful to the following for permission to reproduce copyright materials:

Cover photograph: Bangladesh floods in 1998, courtesy of Shehzad Noorani—Still Pictures/Auscape International.

ANT Photo Library, p. 18 (top); AusAID, p. 12, Michael Jensen/Auscape International, p. 15 (right); Shehzad Noorani—Still Pictures/Auscape International, p. 29 (top); Australian Picture Library/Corbis, p. 18 (bottom); Daniel Buckles, Sierra de Santa Marta, Veracruz, Mexico, p. 13; Coo-ee Picture Library, pp. 4–5 (center); Virginia Elliot, p. 17; Getty Images, pp. 6, 10 (bottom), 11, 16 (bottom), 25 (left), 27 (top); Neil McLeod, p. 7 (top); Brian Parker, pp. 15 (left), 21 (bottom), 26 (bottom); Reuters, pp. 23 (bottom), 28, 29 (bottom); Susan Watson, pp. 4 (far left), 4 (center left), 4 (center right), 4 (far right), 19, 20, 21 (top), 30; World Vision, pp. 22, 24.

While every care has been taken to trace and acknowledge copyright, the publisher tenders their apologies for any accidental infringement where copyright has proved untraceable. Where the attempt has been unsuccessful, the publisher welcomes information that would redress the situation.

Please note
At the time of printing, the Internet addresses appearing in this book were correct. Owing to the dynamic nature of the Internet, however, we cannot guarantee that all these addresses will remain correct.

Global citizens

citizen
a person who lives in a large group of people who they mix with

environments
natural and built surroundings

A global citizen is a person who:
◎   has rights and responsibilities
◎   acts in a caring way based on knowledge and understanding
◎   relates to others within their family, friendship groups, community, and country
◎   develops personal values and commitments
◎   develops a sense of their own role in the world.

A study of global citizenship will help you understand how people affect the quality of global environments and the well-being of others. Active global citizens do not just sit back and wait for others to do something. They turn their ideas into action. Action can take many forms:
◎   volunteering by giving time, help, and ideas freely
◎   talking to your friends
◎   thinking deeply
◎   learning more
◎   taking part in community events.

Throughout this book Harry, Allira, Lin, and Denzel will tell you their ways of acting as global citizens. We can all care for each other and our environment.

ALLIRA

Hi! I'm Allira. I live in a country town near the sea. My family background is Aboriginal–Australian.

HARRY

Hello. I'm Harry. I live with my family in a suburb of a big modern city of four million people.

we are global citizens

In all countries of the world—even in the richer nations—there are groups of people who live in poverty. Poverty can mean:

◎ hunger and thirst
◎ unsafe water
◎ low-standard housing
◎ being sick and not being able to get medical help
◎ not being able to go to school
◎ not knowing how to read and do math
◎ not having a job
◎ living from day to day with little hope for a better future
◎ not having the power to change things.

Global citizens are aware of the differences in people's lives in:

◎ their own neighborhood
◎ their country
◎ the wider world.

For the world to become a fairer place for all to live in, action is needed. Global citizens can act to help improve the quality of life for others.

There are differences in the quality of people's lives around the world. Global citizens try to help change conditions like this and make life better for others.

We are global citizens

LIN

I'm Lin. I migrated to my new country with my parents. We live with my grandparents who came 15 years ago from Malaysia.

DENZEL

Hi! I'm Denzel. My mom and I live in a high-rise apartment close to the city center. We're African-American.

Standards of everyday living

People's quality of life is measured by their standard of living. If people have a good standard of living, their basic needs and also their wants are met.

standard of living
everyday living conditions in a community

The things people need

All people have basic needs that must be met so that they can survive. The basic needs are:
◎ enough healthy food
◎ access to fresh, safe water
◎ clean air to breathe
◎ satisfactory housing.
If people have these, they have a basic standard of living.

The things people want

Beyond their basic needs, most people have things that they want. Wants make their life healthier, safer, and more comfortable. These are some wants:
◎ access to health services
◎ educational and work opportunities
◎ a safe place to live
◎ enough money to buy more than basic food and clothes
◎ being able to go to places for enjoyment and relaxation.

All people have the basic needs of being able to drink clean, safe water and eat healthy food.

Most people want things to make their life more comfortable and enjoyable.

Causes of hunger

Hunger is a problem all over the world. There are more than 800 million people who are hungry. There are hungry people in every country. However, most hungry people live in developing countries, especially in much of Africa, and parts of Asia and Central America.

Because there is so much hunger, we could think that there are problems in producing enough food for everyone. This is a myth. There are some other myths about hunger. These show that poverty is usually the main cause of hunger, not other reasons.

myth
something that is imagined and not based on fact

famine
a widespread, extreme shortage of food

monoculture
a single crop that is farmed over a huge area

Myth	Fact
Not enough food is produced in the world to feed everyone.	The world produces enough grain, vegetables, fruits, nuts, and meat, to supply each person in the world with 3,000 calories (12,500 kJ) a day. This is equal to what an average North American eats daily. There is enough food. The problem is that many people are too poor to pay the price of the available food.
Hunger is caused by famine and natural disasters that cannot be controlled by people.	Natural disasters make news headlines. People could still eat when they occur if there was enough food in storage nearby. Some famines are the result of people at war, not things in nature. Poor people do not have the money to buy nutritious food, nor the resources (land, water, and machinery) to grow enough.
Hunger is the result of having big families. If people had fewer children they would not be hungry.	Big families are not the cause of hunger. It is usually the other way around. Hunger is one of the reasons poor people have lots of children. The more children a poor family has, the more likely some will survive to work in the fields or in the city to add to the family's small income.
Big plantations and farms provide plenty of work and food for poor farmers.	Many farmers who used to grow enough to feed their own family now work on large fields of monoculture. They do not get good wages. They are forced to buy their food and are often too poor to do so.

Poverty means that farmers often do not have modern equipment to produce enough to get them out of poverty.

11

Improving food security

Everybody has the right to food security. Food security means having enough safe and nutritious food for a healthy and active life. This depends on three things:

1   that food is **available**. Adequate amounts of good-quality, safe food must be produced or bought by a country for its people.
2   that food is **accessible**. People must be able to get food locally and be able to afford to buy it.
3   that food is **used** in the best way possible. Food has to be of good enough quality for each person to be healthy.

Global citizens are helping

Over the last 20 to 30 years, some people and countries have been working to improve their food security. During this time, the total number of people living in hunger has fallen by 150 million because of global citizens working together. But many people still do not have enough to eat. There is still more work to do to improve their quality of life.

CASE STUDY **Controlling pests in Indonesia's rice fields**

Pests are always a big problem for farmers everywhere. In Indonesia, farmers have been growing rice for more than 3,000 years. In recent years, chemicals were introduced to kill insect pests. Many of these chemicals damage the soil.

The Australian government, through its international aid program AusAID, has helped the Indonesian government set up Farmers Field Schools. The rice farmers learn how to grow their crops in environmentally responsible ways. This includes learning how to manage pests without using harmful chemicals.

Local people help gather pests in the rice fields so that they can study them. They observe nature, try out different ways of controlling pests, and share their ideas and knowledge. This is helping their food security.

Natural methods are helping

The food security of many communities in Central and South America is also being helped. Farmers are using natural methods to turn poor soil into good soil.

 CASE STUDY **The Magic Mucuna Bean**

In Central America poor farmers cut down and burn the rich forest to get more land to grow things. The land begins to lose its richness when it is cleared. The soil cannot hold water and is washed or blown away.

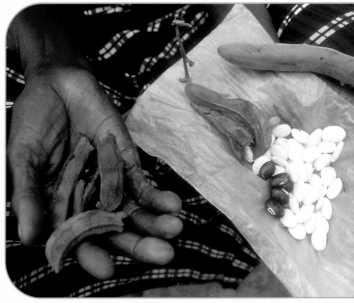

This is where the mucuna bean is helping the problem. Farmers first plant mucuna beans on the cleared land. They produce masses of green growth. The beans are left to rot on the land and maize (a grain like corn) is planted into them. The beans and maize then grow together.

Mucuna produces about 45 tons (41 t) of natural fertilizer per acre, creating rich soils on rocky hillsides in just two or three years. The land never needs to be plowed. It also limits weeds. As the soil improves, the amount of maize harvested is doubled and even tripled.

Guinope is a small town in the Central American country of Honduras. Twenty years ago, Guinope was a dying community. Many of the farmers gave up the struggle to feed their families and went to the cities. Today, some of them are returning to their deserted land. They are using the mucuna bean to turn their farms into land able to grow good-quality food. It does not cost much to start using the mucuna and it pays for itself in a very short time.

What can I do?

Some of my friends and I are going to get more involved in food issues. For World Food Day on October 16, we'll display our school projects and reports about world food security in community spaces.

Fresh, safe water

Water covers three-quarters of Earth's surface. Earth's water consists of:

- ◎ 97 percent salty seawater
- ◎ 2 percent frozen freshwater in polar lands and glaciers
- ◎ 1 percent freshwater in rivers and underground water basins.

It is the 1 percent of freshwater that is precious. It is necessary for the survival of all living things.

Freshwater is scarce. People are using more and more water every day. This is because the world's population is growing. Water is also used in factories and for comforts such as swimming pools and cooling systems. There are some countries that are already facing a water crisis, and many of these are the poorer countries.

Freshwater must be safe if it is to be used by people. Water that looks drinkable can contain harmful things, which cause illness and death. Poor sanitation is one of the main causes of water pollution.

Diarrhea is the second biggest killer of children in the world. It is spread in polluted water.

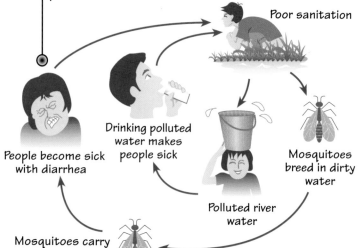

Poor sanitation

Drinking polluted water makes people sick

People become sick with diarrhea

Polluted river water

Mosquitoes breed in dirty water

Mosquitoes carry disease and bite people

sanitation
clean and safe removal of human and household waste by water and drains

Many countries are likely to be short of water by 2025.

KEY
Chance of water shortage in 2025

| None | Low | Medium | High | No data |

People without water

More than one billion people in the world do not have safe drinking water. Most of these people are in developing countries. This contrasts to developed countries where nearly everyone has access to fresh, safe water.

The main reasons for people not having enough safe water are:

◎ **Poverty**—Poor countries and regions cannot afford to build water treatment plants and pipelines.

◎ **Pollution**—Rivers are easily polluted. Water that runs off the land into rivers and lakes can be full of waste from animals and chemicals from fertilizers. Many people use rivers for washing themselves, their clothes, and their animals. Sewage waste is often dumped directly into rivers without treating it first.

◎ **Political reasons**—Huge dams have been built to store water for city people. These dams can rob people outside cities of river water they used to have. Countries can also control the flow of rivers through other countries by building dams and keeping most of the water to themselves.

◎ **Disasters**—Natural disasters such as earthquakes, tornadoes, floods, and volcano eruptions can damage water supply pipes.

water treatment plants
places where water is stored and treated with chemicals to make it clean

pollution
dirty or dangerous conditions that make a part of the environment unclean and unsafe

Many people live in conditions of poverty where they have to walk a long way to collect freshwater.

Pollution of rivers through poor sanitation and people's use harms the access to fresh, safe water.

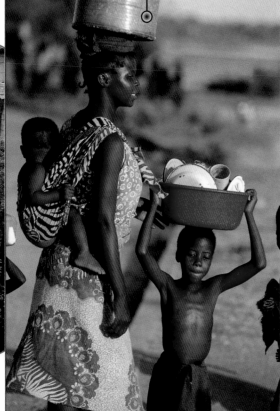

15

irrigation
large-scale watering of farmland by artificial means through channels and sprinklers

World water usage

People use water every day without even thinking where it came from and where it goes. Many people do not value water enough and use it carelessly. Some activities use large amounts of water.

Category	Activities that use water
Households	drinking, cooking, washing, sewerage, watering, filling swimming pools
Industry	for running machinery and cooling in factories
Farming	irrigation of crops and farmland
Energy	making hydro-electricity from water falling through giant engines
Recreation	fishing, swimming, boating

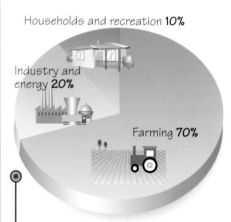

Households and recreation 10%

Industry and energy 20%

Farming 70%

The use of water by the broad types of human activities.

In general, developed countries use far more water than developing countries. On average, Americans use 219 gallons (830 l) of water a day for cooking, washing, flushing, and watering purposes. The average family turns on the faucet between 70 and 100 times daily. Water usage in North and Central America is twice that of Europe, three times that of Asia, and seven times that of Africa.

These huge sprinklers are irrigating crops. Irrigating farmland uses much more water than any of the other activities that people do.

Global citizens watch water

If people do not have enough water, the quality of their lives will get worse. Everyone needs to become more water-wise to help save the world's water. Here are a few ways:

◎ Before turning on the faucet, think carefully about how the water will be used and how much is really needed.

◎ Turn all faucets to low pressure.

◎ Use a container when cleaning rather than a running faucet.

◎ Encourage family and friends to do the same things.

◎ Join a community group and help check water quality in the local area.

◎ Take part in clean-ups to help prevent pollution of freshwater.

GLOBAL FACT

World Water Day is on March 22 each year. The aim is to get people thinking about and acting on the global water problem.

CASE STUDY — Watching water in the local area

There are community action groups that check water quality. They bring together schools and communities. Water bugs, frogs, algae, and habitats are checked to see how healthy the waterways are. The results are put into a database.

The data helps the groups act. They organize awareness campaigns, creek clean-ups, wetland renewal, and talk to industries that use water. Drain stenciling is also becoming popular. People paint words in large letters on the sides of stormwater drains. The messages tell where the water in the drains goes, such as "This water empties into Deep Ponds Lake." Stenciling helps people stop polluting once they know what happens to the water.

What can I do?

Water is cool. But it's also precious. The world might run out of fresh, safe water one day if we don't all start taking action now. I'm going to start being more water-wise in my everyday living.

Air quality at risk

emissions
fumes from gases that are produced from burning, especially carbon dioxide

toxic
poisonous

Most people do not think about the air we breathe. We cannot see, feel, or smell fresh, clean air, but we do know that it makes us feel good. Air contains lots of different gases. The most important gas for us to live is oxygen. We can live for some days without water and food. Without oxygen, we would all be dead in a few minutes!

The air is in danger of being spoiled by pollution. When the quality of the air is spoiled, this affects the quality of people's lives. Air moves around the globe, so the pollution can move from one place to another.

The emissions from burning fuels in motor vehicles, homes, and factories are a major cause of pollution in the air. Burning wood and charcoal in fireplaces and grills also releases large quantities of soot into the air. Soot is a fine, black powder.

Smog is a common type of large-scale outdoor pollution. It is a brownish-yellow haze of smoke and fumes caused by chemical reactions between car exhaust and factory emissions, particularly over big cities. Dangerous fumes can be released from many of the chemicals that people use in factories, fertilizers, and pesticides. Fumes are also released when garbage starts rotting. If the mountain of garbage is very big and dirty, the fumes can be toxic.

Smog is likely to occur on windless days over large cities with lots of cars and factories.

Huge garbage piles give off toxic fumes that add to air pollution and can reduce people's quality of life.

Protecting air quality

Countries can help improve the quality of the air by making laws to control pollution. Many governments have a special department known as the "Environment Protection Authority" or "EPA." The EPA is responsible for making factories and motor vehicle transportation keep to the laws. The EPA can impose fines on any person or business that causes pollution.

Another important action by governments is to give money to tree-planting programs. People have been cutting down more and more trees to burn for fuel, to clear land for settlement, and to use in making buildings. Trees need to be replaced to help the air stay clean. They soak up carbon dioxide, which can harm the air. Trees also produce oxygen during photosynthesis.

GLOBAL FACT

If a person takes a deep breath of air and can smell something, it is air pollution. Clean air has no odor.

photosynthesis
the change of carbon dioxide and water to oxygen and sugars in plants

Fresh, clean air adds to the quality of people's lives.

Global citizens help keep the air clean

It is not only governments that help keep the air clean. Global citizens can take action in their everyday lives that will help. Global citizens can:

◎ stop burning off grass around the garden
◎ walk, bike, or take public transportation to save burning fuel in cars
◎ use less electricity if it is produced from fossil fuels.

What can I do?

I'm going to try to get my family to use our car less. We only need to do one big shopping trip a week with the car. The rest of the time we can walk to buy smaller things, to go the park, and to visit our cousins 10 streets away. We could even take the train next time we want to go into the city.

Differences in housing quality

Housing allows people to live together in family groups. Households create waste. Sanitation removes household waste in a hygienic way.

There are many different types of houses. They vary because of:

◎ the climate

◎ the types of building materials available

◎ whether they are in a crowded city or the open space of the countryside

◎ what people can afford.

Rural living

rural
in the countryside away from cities

Life in rural areas varies from country to country, and from region to region. Some people live in comfortable houses on modern farms or in country towns with good facilities. These people are called the "rural rich."

There are 1.2 billion (1,200,000,000) people living in extreme poverty. Three-quarters of these live in rural areas. They are the "rural poor." They often do not own land and have inadequate housing without power, running water, and sanitation.

The quality of life for the rural poor is limited, especially if they are a long way from towns or cities. They cannot get many of the services they need, such as schools, doctors, and hospitals.

The "rural rich" live in modern houses on productive farmland. They have a good quality of life.

Many women in rural areas of developing countries have to run the house without husbands and brothers when men leave to fight in wars or find paid work in cities. Poor rural women often live in inadequate housing and can never get out of these conditions.

There are differences in the types of housing that people can afford. Many people live in very poor housing conditions.

Urban living

Urban living does not always mean that people have adequate housing and sanitation. More and more people are living in cities. Some rural people move to cities in search of work and better facilities. Other people move from one city to another because they think it offers a better life.

In many cities, there is not enough space for everyone to have adequate housing because:

◎ more than one family often lives together in cramped high-rise apartments

◎ people build rough houses from what materials they can find, creating shanty towns

◎ slums develop where people are too poor to repair them.

People living in poor housing usually try to get paid work to help improve their quality of life. But many never succeed and remain poor all of their lives.

Homeless people

A person of any age could have a poor quality of life because they have no home at all. Young, homeless people are called "street kids." There are homeless people in most countries, even the rich ones. They could be too poor to have permanent homes or have no one to care for them. Some people look down on the homeless if they are forced to beg for money or food.

urban
cities and towns

shanty towns
areas of very poor housing conditions next to better housing in a city

slums
run-down areas of a city with poor houses that are usually overcrowded

GLOBAL FACT

More than 100 million people in the world are homeless.

What can I do?

Our local Salvation Army runs a shelter for homeless people. I'll ask Mom or Dad to come with me to volunteer some time there.

Health services

Health care affects the quality of life

Everybody has the right to lead a healthy life. As well as nutritious food, safe water, clean air, and adequate housing, people need health care. Health services add to the quality of people's lives. They consist of:

◎ doctors and nurses
◎ medical clinics and hospitals
◎ good quality medicines
◎ ambulances and other emergency vehicles
◎ infant child-care clinics
◎ aged-care facilities
◎ medical technology
◎ family planning
◎ immunization programs
◎ health education.

In many countries, the best health services are found in cities. There are fewer health services in rural areas.

family planning medical advice about the size and timing of families

immunization medicine given to prevent disease

Women's health

In developing countries, women in particular are affected by poor health services, especially in rural areas. Every year, more than half a million women die when they are pregnant or in childbirth. Most of these women are poor.

Women's risk of dying in pregnancy or childbirth	
Region	**Risk of dying**
Africa	1 in 16
Asia	1 in 65
South America and Caribbean	1 in 130
Europe	1 in 1,400
North America	1 in 3,700
All developing countries	*1 in 48*
All developed countries	*1 in 1,900*

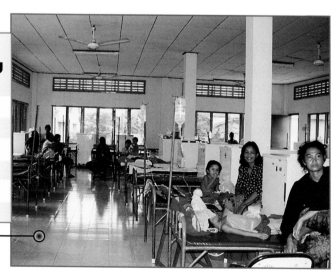

There are differences in the level of health services available in the world. All countries have hospitals but they are mostly found in cities.

Infant mortality

The chances of surviving to your fifth birthday depend on where you are born in the world. Infant mortality is higher in developing countries than developed countries.

The main reasons for this are:

◎ a shortage of medical services
◎ mothers having a large number of children
◎ poor nutrition of mothers and babies
◎ less knowledge of health matters
◎ dirty water supplies.

Infant mortality is mostly due to infectious diseases such as pneumonia, diarrhea, and HIV/AIDS, combined with malnutrition.

Percentage of young children who die before the age of 5.

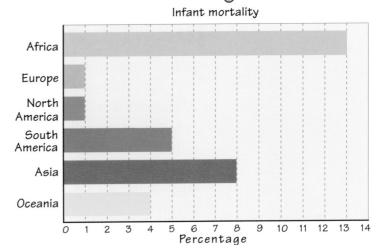

Infant mortality

Life expectancy

Over the last 100 years, people's health opportunities have improved worldwide. Life expectancy has increased in most parts of the world. In 2003, life expectancy in countries such as Canada and the United Kingdom was about 80 years of age. In central and southern Africa, it was only 47, less than it was 10 years earlier. This is because of the HIV/AIDS pandemic, which is more severe in central and southern Africa than anywhere else in the world.

Due to their poor quality of life, many African countries have a life expectancy under 50 years of age.

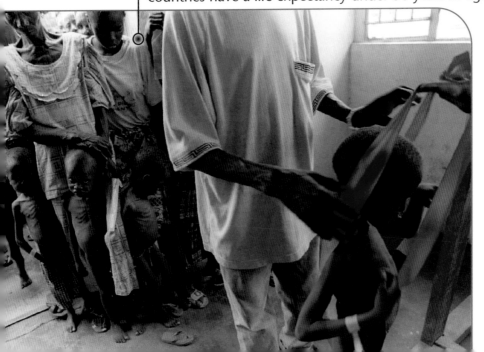

infant mortality
the number of children under the age of 5 who die per 1,000 of population

life expectancy
the average number of years that a person lives

pandemic
an outbreak of a disease that has spread over a large part of the world

GLOBAL FACT

The life expectancy of indigenous Australians (as a group) has not increased in the last 15 years.

Education affects the quality of life

Everybody has the right to a free and basic primary- or elementary-school education and to high school up to age 15. But the full range of education services covers more. Many people have access to:

◎ child-care and nursery schools for infants up to about 5 years of age

◎ primary or elementary schools for children from about 5 years of age to 11 or 12

◎ high schools for young people of 12 to 18

◎ colleges and universities for people who want to continue studying for a career

◎ lifelong learning opportunities for people in areas of personal interest.

Developed countries have more of these services than developing countries. Developed countries usually offer good educational opportunities because of this.

Some developing countries put a very high value on educating their people. However, when there are not enough resources for the whole population, many people miss out. Girls and young women, in particular, might be made to stay at home while boys take up places in schools and colleges.

Educational opportunities can be limited where classrooms are crowded and there are no computers.

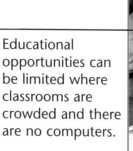

Learning to read and write

It is estimated that 800 million of the world's adults are illiterate. They do not know how to read and write simple statements about everyday life. Nearly 70 percent, or 550 million, are women. Indigenous groups and the rural poor also have low literacy levels.

Illiteracy does not only affect people in developing countries. According to the National Adult Literacy Survey, 40 million adults in the U.S. have low literacy skills. They struggle with reading and helping their children with homework.

There are programs to help adults learn to read and write. These help improve their educational opportunities and the quality of life.

Use of computer technology

There are now many people in the world who have good access to computer technology. Again, these are mostly in developed countries. The gap between rich and poor countries in terms of computer literacy is growing. More than 130 million school-age children in the developing countries do not go to elementary school. Few of these children are able to access books, printed news or computers. Only about 2 out of every 100 people in developing countries have access to computers at all. In countries such as Sweden, the U.S., and Australia, more than 50 out of every 100 people use computers at home and in school.

Computer technology increases people's educational opportunities.

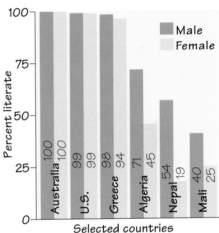

Literacy rates are higher in developed countries.

technology
modern equipment and processes

GLOBAL FACT
International Literacy Day is held on September 8 each year. The aim is to focus on worldwide literacy issues and needs.

What can I do?

Zahra is a new student in our school. She's come from Somalia with her family. She can't read or write English very well yet. I'm going to invite her home sometimes and help her with reading and writing.

Fair pay

People over the age of 15 have the right to a job and to get paid fairly for their work. However, about one billion people do not have the opportunity of such work. This affects one in three people over the age of 15. Having no job, or a poorly paid job, makes it difficult for people to improve their quality of life.

People are sometimes treated as "property" in many parts of the world. This means that wealthier or more powerful people sometimes treat them like slaves. Children and women, in particular, are often forced to work for a master. There are about 250 million child laborers under 15 who are forced to work. Their work conditions are usually very harsh. There are also about 300,000 children who are fighting as soldiers. They have little opportunity to work or train for work.

Women's work

Women's work helps their local economy as well as their country. It adds around 70 percent to the value of an economy. However, they receive less than 10 percent of the world's earnings.

In many countries in Africa and southern Asia, husbands, brothers, and older sons leave their farm villages and families. They try to find paid work in cities. The women and girls are left behind to run the farm as well as raise the children. Most never get paid for this or get any of the money the men might earn. They never have the opportunity to work for a fair wage.

GLOBAL FACT

Workers in developed countries have the opportunity of earning higher wages than those in developing countries.

economy
the level of business activity and wealth in a country

earnings
money made from being in paid work

People's quality of life is affected by having to work in harsh conditions.

Sweatshop conditions

Clothing and footwear companies have brought many new paid jobs to the developing world. Many factories have moved outside the U.S., Canada, Europe, and Australia. This is because the labor is cheaper in developing countries.

    There are no international laws that make these companies provide safe and decent working conditions. They do not have to pay wages that are enough for a family to live on. Workers are forced into sweatshops because there is no other work for them. Sweatshops use labor to do most jobs. They do not have a high use of technology.

international
worldwide

sweatshops
factories where people work in harsh conditions

Technology has changed how people have worked over the past 150 years. This is especially so in the use of computers, satellite equipment, mobile phones, the Internet, and e-mail.

Workers want to be able to improve their quality of life. They want to be paid enough money to survive by their local standards. This is called a living wage. Many workers in developing countries are not earning a living wage. The U.S. National Labor Committee found these rates of pay in clothing and footwear factories:

◎ Chinese workers earn approximately 23 cents per hour, but the living wage in China is 87 cents per hour.
◎ In Haiti, the average worker makes 30 cents per hour, but the living wage is 58 cents per hour.
◎ In Nicaragua, a worker makes only 23 cents per hour, but the living wage is 80 cents per hour.

What can I do?
My country needs to help workers in sweatshop conditions. I'm going to write our local politician. I'll say that there should be some international laws to protect them.

27

Harm caused by people

People can cause dangerous situations. They often result in conflict that harms the quality of life.

Political control

Some governments affect the quality of people's lives by limiting their freedom to speak out and act on issues. Governments can put people in prison and even torture them for acting on their own beliefs.

Discrimination

Discrimination happens when people treat other people unfairly because they are different. Discrimination often leads to violence. People's lives are harmed.

War and terrorism

Although many people live in peaceful communities, there are some countries where war is harming people's lives. In several African countries civil war has continued for more than 20 years.

Lives can also be threatened by terrorist attacks. Small groups who act violently against others, usually for political reasons, are terrorists. Terrorism is part of the violent situation that continues in Northern Ireland and Israel. In the U.S., terrorism was responsible for the attack on the World Trade Center in New York and the Pentagon in Washington on September 11, 2001.

conflict
violent disagreement

civil war
war between different groups within the same country

freedom
not being controlled by others

War and terrorism harm people's quality of life. The attack on New York's World Trade Center on September 11, 2001, was an act of terrorism that killed more than 3,000 people.

Natural disasters

Natural disasters can happen at any time, in any part of the world. They cause death and injury to people and animals, and destruction and damage to houses, roads, crops, and workplaces. They affect people's quality of life.

These are the most common types of natural disasters:

- earthquakes
- floods
- wildfires
- famine
- landslides and mudslides
- hurricanes and tornadoes
- drought
- volcano eruptions
- plagues of pests
- blizzards.

GLOBAL FACT

World Red Cross Day is celebrated on May 8 every year. This is the anniversary of the birth of Henry Dunant, the founder of the Red Cross.

Natural disasters leave people homeless, without running water and food, and likely to catch disease.

relief
help in time of disaster

Global citizens to the rescue

Wherever disaster occurs, there are people and organizations who come to the rescue. They provide relief in the form of shelter, food, and health services. As well as helping victims, they feed emergency workers and handle inquiries from concerned family members.

Relief organizations could not exist without the involvement of thousands of volunteers. Volunteers freely give their time, skills, and energy to helping victims of harmful events. Some of the important international relief organizations are:

- Red Cross and Red Crescent
- Doctors without Borders (Médecins sans Frontières)
- CARE
- World Vision.

Volunteers in international relief organizations help people suffering from a disaster.

Improving the quality of life

We are all citizens of the world. But some of us are more active than others. Global citizens put their ideas into action. Some people think that "action" means protesting or doing something violent. But action can take many forms and can always be peaceful, even in a protest march.

These are some of the actions that global citizens can take to help make a difference in improving people's quality of life:

◎ thinking deeply about issues
◎ volunteering and participating in community activities
◎ helping out wherever you can
◎ standing up for others
◎ joining others on a Web site to lodge petitions with governments
◎ discussing and solving problems in peaceful ways
◎ joining groups that care about the environment and people
◎ using less in your day-to-day life
◎ reusing and recycling.

Global citizens can make a difference so that the quality of people's lives is improved. Remember: an idea is only an idea until someone puts it into action.

What can we do?
Global citizens discuss global issues to try to find ways of solving them. There is hope for the planet if global citizens act together.

citizen a person who lives in a large group of people who they mix with

civil war war between different groups within the same country

conflict violent disagreement

developed countries countries with a high standard of living for most of the people

developing countries countries with much lower living standards than developed countries

earnings money made from being in paid work

economy the level of business activity and wealth in a country

emissions fumes from gases that are produced from burning, especially carbon dioxide

environments natural and built surroundings

family planning medical advice about the size and timing of families

famine a widespread, extreme shortage of food

freedom not being controlled by others

immunization medicine given to prevent disease

infant mortality the number of children under the age of 5 who die per 1,000 of population

international worldwide

irrigation large-scale watering of farmland by artificial means through channels and sprinklers

life expectancy the average number of years that a person lives

malnutrition an illness caused by not having enough healthy food

monoculture a single crop that is farmed over a huge area

myth something that is imagined and not based on fact

natural resources things that occur naturally, which humans can use

pandemic an outbreak of a disease that has spread over a large part of the world

photosynthesis the change of carbon dioxide and water to oxygen and sugars in plants

pollution dirty or dangerous conditions that make a part of the environment unclean and unsafe

poverty extreme lack of money or wealth

poverty cycle a circle of continuing poor quality living from one generation to the next

region a smaller area within a whole country

relief help in time of disaster

rural in the countryside away from cities

sanitation clean and safe removal of human and household waste by water and drains

shanty towns areas of very poor housing conditions next to better housing in a city

slums run-down areas of a city with poor houses that are usually overcrowded

standard of living everyday living conditions in a community

sweatshops factories where people work in harsh conditions

technology modern equipment and processes

toxic poisonous

urban cities and towns

water treatment plants places where water is stored and treated with chemicals to make it clean

wealth the amount of money and resources that a person or country has

Index